make it in
Minutes

Quick & Clever
Gift Wraps

make it in
Minutes

Quick & Clever
Gift Wraps

NICOLE STEIMAN

LARK BOOKS

A Division of Sterling Publishing Co., Inc.,
New York / London

Book Editor

Lecia Monsen

Copy Editors

Lisa Anderson
Catherine Risling

Photographer

Zachary Williams
Williams Visual

Stylist

Brittany Aardema

Book Designer

Kehoe + Kehoe Design
Associates, Inc.

*Other Books
in this Series:*

Make It in Minutes:
Greeting Cards

Make It in Minutes:
Mini-Books

Make It in Minutes:
Mini-Boxes

Make It in Minutes:
Beaded Jewelry

Make It in Minutes:
Party Favors
& Hostess Gifts

Make It in Minutes:
Felt Accessories

Make It in Minutes:
Faux Floral
Arrangements

A Red Lips 4 Courage Communications, Inc. book
www.redlips4courage.com
Eileen Cannon Paulin
President
Catherine Risling
Director of Editorial

Library of Congress Cataloging-in-Publication Data

Steiman, Nicole, 1969-
Make it in minutes : quick & clever gift wraps / Nicole Steiman. – 1st ed.
     p. cm.
Includes index.
ISBN-13: 978-1-60059-202-7 (hc-plc concealed spiral : alk. paper)
ISBN-10: 1-60059-202-3 (hc-plc concealed spiral : alk. paper)
1. Paper work. 2. Gift wraps. I. Title.
TT870.S679 2007
745.54--dc22
                                        2007014724
10 9 8 7 6 5 4 3 2 1

First Edition

Published by Lark Books, A Division of
Sterling Publishing Co., Inc.
387 Park Avenue South, New York, NY 10016

Text ©2007, Nicole Steiman
Photography ©2007, Red Lips 4 Courage Communications, Inc.
Illustrations ©2007, Red Lips 4 Courage Communications, Inc.

Distributed in Canada by Sterling Publishing,
c/o Canadian Manda Group, 165 Dufferin St.
Toronto, Ontario, Canada M6K 3H6

Distributed in the United Kingdom by GMC Distribution Services,
Castle Place, 166 High Street, Lewes, East Sussex, England BN7 1XU

Distributed in Australia by Capricorn Link (Australia) Pty Ltd.,
P.O. Box 704, Windsor, NSW 2756 Australia

If you have questions or comments about this book, please contact:
Lark Books
67 Broadway
Asheville, NC 28801
(828) 253-0467

Manufactured in China

ISBN 13: 978-1-60059-202-7
ISBN 10: 1-60059-202-3

For information about custom editions, special sales, premium and corporate purchases, please contact Sterling Special Sales Department at (800) 805-5489; or e-mail specialsales@sterlingpub.com.

"We make a living by what we get,
we make a life by what we give."
—Sir Winston Churchill

Contents

Introduction

In today's hectic life, gift cards are readily available for practically anything, making giving a present almost too convenient. So what shows the thought you invest in the things you give? I used to think it was because I took time to match a gift to the recipient. However, many times I have found the perfect gift because I asked what the person wanted, checked an online wish list, or found an object circled in a catalog and purchased it. The actual giving was anticlimactic.

I believe the presentation of the gift demonstrates your good wishes nearly as much as what's in the package. Even a last-minute gift card purchase is exciting when it's cleverly wrapped. With the ideas in this book, it may seem like the gift is the wrapping itself. I hope the projects inspire you to create your own unique wrapping creations. Perhaps in giving gifts it is the thought that counts, but it's the wrapping that will win the recipient's heart.

CHAPTER 1

If you love creating things, chances are you have most gift-wrapping supplies already at your fingertips, even though you may not be currently using them to wrap gifts. Mixed media, scrapbooking, quilting, painting, and rubber-stamping supplies can all be used to create unique and clever packages for special occasions.

Gift wrapping is art that you give away, making the creation a celebration all by itself. Look through your office supplies, fabric, and wallpaper scraps, restaurant to-go bags, and even printed papers and charms. Before long you'll be coveting the plain, brown-handled bags at the store just as much as the purchases they contain. So gather your supplies and friends together to have a wrap party that will engage all of your creative juices.

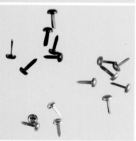

Embellishments

Alcohol ink
This type of ink adheres well to nonporous, slick surfaces. It is packaged in dropper bottles and can be applied directly on surfaces, applied with a felt applicator, or painted on with a brush.

Beads and flat-backed crystals
Almost anything can be decorated by adding beads. Adhere larger beads with strong-hold glue. Smaller beads and flat-backed crystals can be adhered quickly with extra tacky double-sided tape.

Brads
Brads are ideal for wrapping because they not only decorate but also attach and hold wrapping items together. Studs are similar to brads except that they have multiple prongs along the outer edge of the head, which are then pushed through the paper or fabric. Eyelets make interesting lace-up effects for bottles and cylinders, as well as decorated patterns.

Charms
There are a multitude of shaped charms for endless occasions, made of materials ranging from plastic to metal. Adhere charms with a hot-glue gun or clear-drying metal glue. Small flat-backed charms will even stick with extra tacky double-sided tape.

Foil
Metallic and colored foils add a shiny, raised dimension. Foil is a common supply at printer shops and also art supply stores. Adhere it shiny side up to projects using double-sided tape, foiling and glue pens, and even glue sticks.

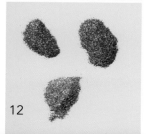

Glitter
Glitter comes in various forms, from superfine to chunky, mica powders, and flakes. Glitter glue has adhesive already mixed with the glitter, which makes it easy to apply. It works particularly well for superfine lines and topcoats, and to create free-form shapes and borders.

Metal leafing

Metal leafing comes in thin sheets or flakes and is generally found in silver, gold, copper, or variegated colors. For fast application, apply leafing to extra tacky double-sided tape and brush off excess flakes. For areas that are not flat enough for tape, use a leafing adhesive.

Metal leafing pens

Metal leafing pens are metal paint in a marker applicator. Just press down on the tip until the paint starts flowing, and then touch up your projects by coloring directly on the item.

Metal sheets

Available in different materials, usually aluminum or copper, metals come in various gauges. Can be embossed, crimped, and even punched with craft punches to make charms. The higher the gauge, the thinner the metal. Use a gauge between 36 and 40 to crimp or emboss designs.

Ribbons

Ribbons come in endless combinations of colors and materials. Common types are satin, grosgrain, and wired and unwired organdy sheer. Generally, the more elaborate the wrapping, the simpler the bow, and the smaller the package, the smaller the ribbon width.

Stencils and templates

Use ready-made stencils or create your own from heavy cardstock or stencil film. Letter and number oil board stencils are available from office supply stores and add an interesting graphic look.

Trims

In addition to ribbons there are countless other interesting trims that can be wrapped around a gift or glued to the center of a bow. Pom-pom fringe, strips of paper, and netting suggest a wide ribbon effect. In addition, bunches of flowers, sprays, seashells, hanging tassels, and feathers are just a few of the add-ons that make great toppers for gifts.

Tools

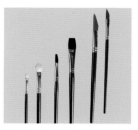

Artist brushes

Bone folder

Bow-making tool

Crimper

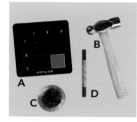

Eyelet setting tools
A Setting mat   C Eyelets
B Craft hammer   D Eyelet setter

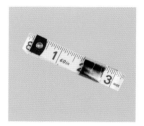

Fabric tape measure

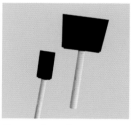

Foam brushes

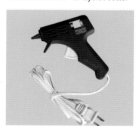

Hot-glue gun

Needle-nose pliers

Paper punches

Piercing tool

Wire cutters

Techniques

Applying alcohol ink

Alcohol inks work best on glossy, nonporous surfaces, which allows the paint to float on the surface. This floating quality of the ink allows you to create color blending. For more floating, apply a blending solution before painting and also during the application for interesting effects. Inks can be dropped right out of the dropper bottles or sponged on with a felt applicator. The metallic paint of leafing pens acts as a resist to the inks, causing veining that resembles marbling. Applying alcohol inks is a quick way to create an elegant painted surface on a metal object, such as a tin flower can or mint tin. Just dab the color and leafing pen right onto the felt, and then quickly sponge onto the project surface.

Applying foil

Foil provides metallic accents and is usually found on a roll or packaged in small sheets. Although commercial printers use hot press machines to create these shiny, raised accents, it is very easy and fun to do using basic tools. To apply random highlights of foil, simply swipe a glue stick around the edges or across the top of your paper and before the glue dries, place a sheet of foil, shiny side up, on top of it; rub firmly, and then lift the sheet. Because of the quick-drying nature of a glue stick, some parts of the foil will stick while others won't, creating a random effect that looks great, especially around edges of photos. If you want the foil to stick more thoroughly, use a foiling pen. Simply write a word, draw a picture, or accent a patterned paper. The glue will appear tinted blue when it first comes out. Let the glue dry until it is tacky and clear. Then press your foil down, shiny side up, and lift. Micro-fine glitters and leafing metals also adhere easily to foiling pens.

Setting studs

Place paper or fabric right side up on top of a thick foam cushion. Place stud in desired location, push firmly through paper or fabric, and then lift out of the foam and turn material over to the back side. Using the flat edge of a bone folder, bend each prong toward the center of the stud. If you are setting a large number of studs, there are setters that make the process seamless. Simply follow the manufacturer's instructions.

time-saving tip

Sealing Wax

Sealing wax is an elegant way to close an envelope flap or hold a ribbon or feather in place. Use real wax sticks that contain a little polymer for flexibility. This will ensure that the wax does not get too brittle and crack when mailing or being handled.

Stamping with bleach

Creating your own patterned papers is easy by using pre-made stamp designs. Instead of inkpads, try making your own bleach pad by carefully pouring undiluted bleach onto a sponge set in a tray or on a plate. Stamp in the same manner as with an inkpad. After stamping, allow time for the bleach effect to appear. Make sure to dispose of your sponge afterward. For safer options, you can also purchase inkpads that mimic the effects of bleach or create a watermark effect.

Wrapping neatly and crisply

Anyone can wrap paper around something and tape it. Make your gift wrapping look more professional by cutting the appropriate amount of paper; extra paper creates a bulky, sloppy look. Cut enough paper to wrap around the width of the box, plus 2"–4" more for the seam. For the ends of the box, cut paper long enough to equal the length of the box, plus one and a half times the box height. Use a measuring tape or marked string, or simply unroll the paper and cut using the package on top as a guide. Use double-sided tape under the edges that you secure rather than cellophane tape on top. Before taping down paper edges, fold them under to make a straight, crisp edge. When wrapping paper around a box, make the seam fall on the edge of the package or meet in the middle where you can cover it with ribbon. After wrapping, create crisp edges by running a thumb and forefinger along all the edges of the package, pinching them around the corners to create a tightly wrapped look.

Ribbon Bow Guidelines

As a general rule, the lighter or thinner the ribbon you use, the more loops your bow should have, usually 6–12 per side. And the heavier and wider the ribbon, the longer your loops should be, approximately 2"–6".

Use this easy calculation to figure how much ribbon your bow will need. Amount of ribbon = 2 x (bow loop size) x (total amount of loops, both sides) + length of tails on each side. For example, a bow with twelve 3" loops will require 84" of ribbon (2 x 3 x 12 + 12 = 84). In other words, twelve 6" loops of ribbon, plus a 6" tail on each side. When at all possible, use ribbon off the bolt to allow for slight variations in the loop size.

Wrapping ribbon around a gift

One common way to use ribbon on a present is to wrap it around all four sides, crossing underneath, and finally tying it in a shoelace bow on top. This is usually accomplished by flipping the box upside down and criss-crossing both ends of the ribbon, causing a section of twisted ribbon on the bottom of the gift. It's not a bad method, but who wouldn't want a flatter bottom? Following are a few refinements that will make your tied package look better and give it a less bulky bottom. Note: An added advantage to this technique is that you can leave the ribbon on the bolt, or figure out the needed length of ribbon by measuring around both sides of the box and adding either 24" for a shoelace bow or 8" for a simple knot.

When the instructions refer to the top of the box, it is the side you see when looking down from above.

Wrapping ribbon around a gift

Fig. 1

Hold one end of ribbon on top center of the gift box with your thumb. Wrap remaining ribbon vertically around box back to top (Fig. 1).

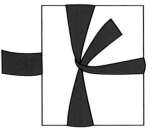

Fig. 2

Wrap longer ribbon length around shorter ribbon in a 90-degree angle and around the side, under box and back to top (Fig. 2).

Fig. 3

Tuck long end of ribbon over and then under ribbon twist made in previous step 2 (Fig. 3).

Fig. 4

Knot ribbon ends and then tie in a shoelace bow; trim to desired length (Fig. 4).

17

Making Bows

There are many types of bows, but knowing just a few elegant ones will enable you to create the perfect embellishment for any gift, whether it's a box, bag, or bottle. *Note:* For many of the following instructions, you will need to use ribbon off a bolt rather than a specified length and then cut the ribbon once the bow is complete.

Shoelace bow
The shoelace bow is the most common type of bow found on a gift and is named after the bow you tie on your shoe. Extra ribbons in various textures and colors can be tied onto the base of the bow to make it more decorative.

Shoelace bow

Fig. 1

Wrap ribbon around the gift and tie a half-knot to secure, leaving a tail at least 10". From starting knot, form equal length loops with each ribbon end (Fig. 1).

Fig. 2

Cross right loop over left loop, forming an X. Wrap top of right loop down over left loop, aiming for the hole in the bottom of the X (Fig. 2).

Fig. 3

Thread right loop through hole (Fig. 3).

Fig. 4

Pull loops tight, forming a bow; adjust as needed (Fig. 4). Trim tails to desired length.

Florist bow

Florist bows have a variety of loops in graduated sizes. The loops are wired together and then spread apart to make a rounded shape with hanging tails. Bow-making devices are very helpful when making these types of bows because they hold the loops together while you secure them with wire. Although more expensive, wired ribbon is also very useful to help the loops hold a more pronounced shape. *Note:* Tying this bow takes some experience, so it's a good idea to practice making a few before creating one for your gift.

Florist bow

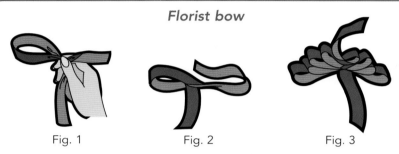

Fig. 1 Fig. 2 Fig. 3

Pinch the ribbon and form a loop, leaving desired length of ribbon for one bow tail (Fig. 1). Make same-size loop in the opposite direction (Fig. 2).

Continue adding loops on each side, securing them under thumb and forefinger, decreasing loop lengths for each layer (Fig. 3).

Fig. 4

Fig. 5

Once you have desired number of loops, twist one last small loop around your thumb to make center loop (Fig. 4). Insert floral wire through center loop and twist tightly on bow back, securing all loops. Fluff out bow, starting with bottom two loops.

Pull loops tightly in opposite directions. Continue with remaining loops until you have desired bow shape (Fig. 5). Trim tails to desired length using an angled cut. To create a forked cut, fold end of ribbon in half lengthwise and cut at an angle toward folded edge.

CHAPTER 2

From birthdays to holidays and all the special occasions in between, there are so many opportunities to give gifts all year long. Use the gift-wrapping ideas in this chapter to turn everyday gift boxes into wrappings that reflect the uniqueness of the recipient and the occasion. Bring a box wrapped in glass gems to a girl's night out, a puzzle gift box to a retirement celebration, or an elegant wallpaper-wrapped gift to a wedding. In this chapter you'll also find some clever uses of everyday materials, such as hardware masking paper. Although you may have wrapped hundreds of gifts before, you may have never thought to stamp paper with bleach or tear up those old jeans sitting in the back of your closet. These unique ideas make wrapping more than an everyday task.

Birthday Baubles

Materials

- Adhesives: dimensional glossy glue, double-sided tape
- Gift box
- Glass pebbles: $3/8$" clear flat-backed
- Kraft paper
- Ribbon: 2" wired sheer light blue
- Scissors

Instructions

1. Wrap box in kraft paper, securing edges with double-sided tape.

2. Apply dot of dimensional glossy glue to center back of glass gem and press onto kraft paper. Repeat randomly across entire top of package. Wait a few minutes, and then turn to another side. Repeat for all remaining sides.

3. Wrap wired ribbon around package and tie in a shoelace bow. Shape wire as desired.

time-saving tip

Gluing on Porous Papers

This technique will not work well on glossy papers because the glue will have nothing porous to soak into. Although glass usually only adheres with super glue, the porous quality of kraft paper creates a nice bond that allows you to move to the next side almost as soon as you finish with the first.

The Bird & The Ivy

Materials

- Adhesives: double-sided tape, hot-glue gun
- Bleach
- Disposable foam plate
- Disposable gloves
- Feathered bird: light peach
- Florist wire
- Gift box: small enough to fit masking paper width
- Masking paper: 12"-wide roll
- Pearl strand
- Ribbon: 2¼" ivory satin wired, 1½" ivory sheer
- Rubber stamp: large swirl
- Scissors
- Sponge

Instructions

1. Roll out length of masking paper long enough to wrap gift box.

2. Set sponge on foam plate and carefully pour ½ cup of bleach onto sponge. Using sponge as an inkpad and wearing gloves, press stamp evenly onto sponge, coating entirely with bleach, and then press onto masking paper. Rotate stamp at various angles each time you stamp to vary design. Wash stamp thoroughly immediately after stamping and dispose of gloves. Let paper dry about 5 minutes. *Note:* The bleached design will gradually change to a peach color.

3. Wrap gift box using double-sided tape. *Note:* Depending on the size of the gift box, you may need to place longer boxes lengthwise on paper and fold up side flaps on long end of box.

4. Wrap ribbon diagonally around opposite corners and tie in knot on top of one corner.

5. Create florist bow with wired ivory satin ribbon, ivory sheer ribbon, and pearl trim. Make eight 3" loops on each side of ivory wired ribbon, three 3" loops on each side of ivory sheer ribbon, and two 3" loops on each side of pearl strand. Wire bow onto ribbon knot.

6. Adhere bird in front of bow using hot-glue gun. Drape 18" length of pearl trim through bow and glue in place.

Gold Glamour

Materials

- Costume jewelry brooch
- Craft knife
- Craft wire
- Foam brush
- Gift box
- Leafing sealer
- Metallic leaf flakes
- Metallic tassel
- Ribbon: ¼" double-faced satin ribbon (4½'), 3" metallic brocade (24")
- Rubber gloves
- Ruler
- Scissors
- Spray leafing adhesive

Instructions

1. Remove lid from box. Spray outside of lid and box with leafing adhesive.

2. Wearing rubber gloves, apply metallic leaf flakes over adhesive using foam brush and fingers. When dry, smooth flakes with brush. Spray box with leafing sealer; let dry.

3. Using craft knife, make two 1" slits in center of box lid in the pattern of a cross. Place lid on box.

4. Cut ribbon into two 12" pieces. Wrap ribbons around box, tucking in slits in center of box lid.

5. Wrap ¼" ribbon in ten 5" loops. Wrap craft wire around center of loops. Insert wire ends into slit in center of lid.

6. Attach tassel to bottom of brooch. Pin brooch to ribbons where they meet at center of box.

Puzzle

Materials

- Adhesives: ¼" tacky tape, craft glue, glue stick, spray adhesive
- Craft knife
- Foam brush
- Gift box
- Papers: black kraft, corrugated cardboard
- Pencil
- Puzzle book
- Ribbon: ⅝" black grosgrain
- Ruler
- Scissors

Instructions

1. Cut length of corrugated cardboard long enough to wrap box. Cut piece of black kraft paper slightly smaller than cardboard so it doesn't extend past cardboard edges when folded. Apply spray adhesive to black kraft paper and lay cardboard on top with corrugated texture facing up. Let dry until tacky, about 10–15 minutes.

2. Wrap gift with layered paper, corrugated side facing out. Adhere sides with tacky tape.

3. Cut 2" square of cardboard to use as template. On corrugated box, trace around template with craft knife, creating random windows as desired. Be careful to only cut through cardboard layer. Remove cardboard layer to reveal black kraft paper underneath.

4. Cut out puzzles from puzzle book to fit in windows. Adhere using glue stick.

5. Glue portions of incomplete puzzles around pencil using craft glue. Brush more craft glue over top to seal; let dry.

6. Wrap ribbon around package and knot, leaving long tails for bow. Tie shoelace bow around pencil. Trim ribbon tails as desired.

Picnic

Materials

- Adhesives: craft glue, hot-glue gun
- Bone folder
- Embellishments: plastic fork and spoon, shipping tag with string
- Fabrics: 17" square, 11" square, coordinating dark red/ivory pattern (1 each)
- Foam brush
- Gable box: 9" x 6"
- Inkpad: midnight blue
- Ladybug: papier-mâché
- Old pair of denim jeans with back pocket
- Ribbons: coordinating colors and patterns (12" each)
- Ruler
- Scissors
- Sewing needle
- Star studs (9)
- Trim: ½" denim with silver rings (32")

Instructions

1. Cut two 8½" x 5½" pieces of one fabric and two 5½" squares of second fabric. Using sewing needle, fray all edges.

2. Flatten gable box and brush craft glue completely on one large side. Center large piece of fabric; press down and smooth. Repeat on opposite large side.

3. Center and adhere three star studs on center of both fabric squares, using bone folder to flatten prongs on reverse side. Adhere embellished fabric on box ends.

4. Measure around top edge of box and cut length of trim to fit. Adhere to box using hot-glue gun.

5. Cut off top layer of back pocket from jeans, without side seams. Using needle, fray top of pocket. Fold in bottom and sides of pocket to re-create pocket shape. Secure each folded edge with hot-glue gun. Embellish pocket with three star studs. Adhere pocket to center front of long side of box.

6. Cut two ½" x 12" denim strips from legs of jeans and fray edges as desired. Open box and tie denim strips and ribbons around handle. Rub inkpad along box edges as desired. Adhere ladybug to bottom edge of pocket using hot-glue gun. Insert shipping tag and plastic cutlery inside pocket.

Candy Curls

Materials

- Adhesives: double-sided tape, foam dots
- Candy: wrapped taffy squares
- Gift box
- Paper: purple striped
- Plastic balloon cluster party favors (5)
- Ribbons: yellow curling (10'), ⅛" pink (1 yard)
- Scissors

Instructions

1. Wrap gift with purple paper.

2. Cut two lengths of curling ribbon and wrap around width and length of present, knotting at top. Attach balloon party favor clusters in middle of knot by wrapping favor wire around ribbon. Arrange as desired.

3. Curl length of curling ribbon, 12" at a time, by running ribbon across edge of scissors. Gather curls into mound and tuck in between balloons, draping as desired. *Note:* Don't cut the ribbon into shorter lengths. The mound is one long, curled ribbon.

4. Adhere two square candies, sandwich-style, onto either side of pink ribbon every 2" using foam dots. Drape embellished pink ribbon across top of present by tucking into balloons to secure as needed. Repeat with additional candy ribbons as desired. *Note:* The weight of the candy ribbon will hold the mound of curling ribbon in place.

time-saving tip

Good Enough to Eat

Kids love colorful packages with lots of curling ribbon, and lots of candy doesn't hurt either. If you're short on time, just adhere various candy bars and colorful bags of candy randomly to the wrapped gift using foam dots. For extra fun, top off the package with a birthday hat, securing the elastic chin strap around the present.

Crystal Celebration

Materials

- ¼" tacky tape
- Acrylic paints: red, silver, white
- Artist's brush: 1½"
- Crystal garland (18")
- Florist wire
- Gift box
- Plastic container
- Ribbon: ¾" light pink wired
- Scissors
- Wallpaper: paintable embossed

Instructions

1. Cut section of wallpaper large enough to wrap gift box.

2. Using artist's brush, apply thick coat of silver paint to wallpaper; let dry and then add second coat.

3. Mix drop of red paint in ½ cup of white paint in plastic container to create a very pale pink. Add additional drops of red until desired color is achieved. Lightly brush pink paint only on raised parts of wallpaper as desired; let dry.

4. Wrap gift box in painted wallpaper. Wrap pink ribbon around package and knot on box top. Create florist bow with thirty-two 3" loops. Place crystal garland across knot and wire bow on top.

time-saving tip

Paint the Whole Roll

While you have all your paints out, go ahead and paint the whole roll of wallpaper so it's ready for future gifts. Also, experiment with different paint combinations.

Glittered Snowflakes

Materials

- Acetate: clear adhesive-backed
- Acrylic paints: jewel-toned blue, pearlescent
- Brushes: artist's, foam
- Double-sided tape
- Florist wire
- Glitter: micro-fine silver
- Iron and tea towel
- Jump ring: silver
- Kraft paper
- Needle-nose pliers
- Ornament: silver glittered star
- Punch: 2" snowflake
- Ribbon: 2" wired metallic silver honeycomb
- Scissors

Instructions

1. Cut length of kraft paper large enough to wrap gift. Mix pearlescent and jewel-toned blue paints to create desired color. Brush paint onto paper using artist's brush. Run foam brush over paint as it is drying to smooth out most of brush marks; let dry completely.

2. Iron dry paper on low setting with tea towel between. Wrap present, adhering with double-sided tape.

3. Punch twelve snowflakes from adhesive-backed acetate. Peel off back layer of punched shape to expose adhesive. Sprinkle micro-fine glitter on adhesive; brush off excess. Repeat for remaining snowflakes.

4. Create florist bow with two graduated loops on either side and a small center loop.

5. Wrap ribbon around length of package and secure with tape. Fasten bow on top with wire.

6. Randomly adhere snowflakes, glitter side up, on package. Add star ornament to bow with silver jump ring and pliers.

CHAPTER 3

One of the most versatile wrappings of all, a gift bag is also one of the most fun to embellish. Bags are readily available in different sizes and colors, making it easy to coordinate with your occasion or gift. By removing the handle and replacing it with your own, you can transform a plain bag into something extra special. Use candy necklaces or a flowered lei as an unexpected handle. Even restaurant and shopping bags are transformable with a little paint and unique trim. You'll start looking at your scraps of ribbon and fabric a little differently once you get hooked on creating your own gift bags. And don't stop with the outside of the bag. Nestle your gifts in fabrics like plush felt or earthy burlap, netting, or tissue paper to continue your theme.

Flower Power

Materials

- Adhesives: ¼" tacky tape, hot-glue gun

- Fibers: fuchsia, variegated green

- Flower: fuchsia silk daisy

- Gift bag: 5½"x 8" glossy black

- Hot-glue gun

- Ribbons: ½" black-and-white dot grosgrain, ½" lime green, ⅛" lime satin (various lengths), ½" pink-and-white dot grosgrain

- Scrim: 6"x 3¼" black

- Shredded paper: assorted colors

Instructions

1. Vertically and horizontally, weave ribbons and fibers randomly in and out of scrim, leaving some ribbons dangling on sides.

2. Apply two lines of tacky tape on back side of scrim behind thicker ribbons and adhere to middle of bag. Adhere daisy with hot-glue gun.

3. Insert gift and add shredded paper at top of bag.

time-saving tip

Start a Ribbon Remnant Bag

Here's a reason to save all those luscious snippets of ribbon that get cut off of gifts at bachelorette parties, birthdays, baby showers, and more. Even the smallest remnants can be woven through a few holes in the scrim. Wrap the woven scrim around a wrapped gift box as a fun, funky ribbon. For those who sew and quilt, try it with skinny strips of fabric remnants.

42

Hula

Materials

- Bag: canvas (10" square)
- Flowered lei (36")
- Hot-glue gun
- Raffia: blue, fuchsia, green, golden yellow, natural, orange (¼ bundle each)
- Ruler
- Scissors
- Sewing needle
- Shells: small (12)

Instructions

1. Cut three 36" lengths of natural raffia. Tie ends between two chairs, about 30" apart, and pull raffia taut. Pull out three strands of one color of raffia and fold in half, creating a loop. Wrap loop under string of natural raffia and pull ends up and through loop, like a bookmark tassel. Pull tightly toward the floor. Repeat with various colors until length of natural raffia is covered; trim raffia skirt to desired length.

2. Using hot-glue gun, adhere skirt around canvas bag, right under top seam line.

3. Cut off bag handles using scissors. Cut lei in half and remove 4" of flowers to reveal wire. Thread wire through needle and sew lei to one side of bag where handles were cut. Knot end and add hot-glue to secure. Repeat with remaining three sides. Glue shells on outside of bag to hide sewn spots.

time-saving tip

Wearable Wrapping

Use a real grass skirt from a party supply store and attach it to a larger-sized bag. Baste the skirt onto the bag with thread so that it can be easily removed and worn at a party.

Baby Bib

Materials

- ¼" tacky tape
- Brads: white daisies (6)
- Buttons: small white (2)
- Dimensional stickers: pink baby bib, soft toy
- Felt: white (18")
- Gift bag: 8"x 9½" glossy light pink
- Pencil
- Piercing tool
- Punch: ⅛" hole
- Ribbon: ¼" light pink-and-white gingham (36"), ⅜" pink polka dot grosgrain (8"), 1½" wired baby pink (1 yard)
- Ruler
- Scissors: craft, scallop-edge
- Stencils: 3", 6" circle
- Wallpaper: paintable scallop embossed

Instructions

1. Trace 6" circle using stencil onto wallpaper. Cut out with scallop-edge scissors. Trace bottom half of 3" stencil at top of scalloped circle and cut out with craft scissors, creating bib shape.

2. Punch two holes inside each scallop along edge of bib. Leaving 6" as tail, weave gingham ribbon in and out of punched holes.

3. Cut off bag handles and replace with 18" of wired ribbon on each side. Knot each end inside of bag to secure. Repeat on opposite side.

4. Adhere 8" length of polka dot ribbon along bottom edge of bag with tacky tape. Using piercing tool, make holes and attach daisy brads between polka dots.

5. Attach buttons on each side of bib with tacky tape. Tie bib to bag front around handles. Add a few pieces of tacky tape underneath bib edges to secure, rounding the bib a little rather than taping it flat against the bag.

6. Cut off bib straps from dimensional sticker and place baby toy sticker on top. Secure to bib with tacky tape. Wrap gift in white felt and place in bag.

Graffiti

Materials

- Acrylic paints: cobalt teal, dark violet, gold, green
- Adhesives: ¼" tacky tape, glue stick
- Bag: 16" x 12" kraft
- Cardstock: 8½" x 5½" green
- Chipboard: 4" x 10"
- Foam brush
- Foam stamps: 1½" numbers
- Paint scraper or old credit card
- Paper punch: 1½" circle
- Ruler
- Scissors
- Stencil: 4" letter of choice
- Trim: 2"-wide black belting (1 yard)

Instructions

1. Dip half of scraper in paint color of choice and scrape horizontally, vertically, and diagonally across bag. Repeat with remaining colors of paint; let dry. Edge bag with dark violet paint and foam brush.

2. Brush dark violet paint on back of foam number stamps and press randomly around bag. Repeat to create some green numbers; let dry.

3. Punch six 1½" circles out of green cardstock. Edge with foam brush and dark violet paint; let dry. Adhere columns of three circles along side and middle of bag with glue stick.

4. Sponge all edges of letter stencil with dark violet paint and foam brush. Adhere to bag with glue stick and scrape more paint onto stencil. Using punched cardstock scrap as stencil, sponge dark violet circles randomly on bag with foam brush.

5. Cut handles off bag. Measure and cut 2" x 10" strips of chipboard reinforcement for each side of bag top. Apply several strips of tacky tape to chipboard; secure belting to chipboard, forming a handle. Adhere belting side of chipboard to bag with several strips of tacky tape. Repeat on opposite side.

Batik

Materials

- Craft glue
- Decorative studs: various designs and colors (4)
- Fabric scraps: coordinating colors and patterns
- Gift bag: kraft
- Postage stamps
- Rope: ⅛" braided orange jute
- Ruler
- Scissors: craft, pinking shears

Instructions

1. Cut twenty-one 1"x 1½" fabric swatches with pinking shears.

2. Starting at top left corner of bag, glue swatches, leaving 1" space between. Alternate next row by centering and gluing swatches below spaces. Continue adding rows until bag is covered.

3. Glue length of jute to fill space at bottom. Repeat with additional lengths as needed.

4. Add decorative studs and postage stamps to random swatches.

5. Cut off bag handle. Punch four holes for handles. Braid three 24" strands of jute for front handle. Pull each end of jute through hole and knot. Fray edges of jute. Repeat for back handle.

time-saving tip

Stock Swatch Books

Fabric and wallpaper swatch books are great for this technique, so ask your local design stores when they are ready to toss their old sample books. You can also use snippets of wrapping paper, patterned paper, photos, and greeting cards—another perfect excuse to never throw anything away.

Funky Monogram

Materials

- Acrylic paint: black
- Adhesives: ½" tacky tape, glue stick
- Artist's paintbrush
- Chipboard letter: 8"
- Decorative studs: large antique silver (3)
- Fabric: leopard print fur
- Gift bag: 8" x 9½" glossy black
- Pencil
- Ribbon: ⅝" black acetate (9")
- Scissors
- Tissue paper: zebra pattern

Instructions

1. Lay chipboard letter face-down on wrong side of fur. Trace around letter and cut out.

2. Paint sides of chipboard letter black; let dry.

3. Glue fur cutout to black monogram with glue stick or tacky tape, depending on weight of fabric.

4. Stretch out length of black ribbon on section of letter. Mark to place decorative studs. Attach three studs to black ribbon and fold back prongs using light pressure so ribbon does not pucker.

5. Adhere studded ribbon to letter and then letter to bag using tacky tape. Wrap gift in tissue paper and place in bag.

time-saving tip

Securing Prongs

There are spring-arm machines designed to attach studs by pushing them through a material's surface and bending the prongs back. Use very light pressure when attaching studs to delicate fabric. If you don't have a special machine, simply place the fabric on a foam surface so that when you press in the stud, the prongs will sink through. Lift fabric and stud from foam, turn over, and use flat edge of bone folder to bend each prong back to secure.

Vintage Holiday

Materials

- Adhesives: glue stick, hot-glue gun
- Brads: mini silver (3)
- Charms: silver pinwheels (3)
- Faux berries: small cluster
- Glitter glue: platinum
- Metal sheet: 5" square 38-gauge aluminum
- Paper: antique sheet music
- Piercing tool
- Punch: 1½" snowflake
- Ruler
- Trim: red pompom (8")
- Vintage image

Instructions

1. Tear piece of sheet music to 5½" x 8". Center and adhere to bag using glue stick.

2. Adhere vintage image to left side of sheet music with glue stick. Outline image with glitter glue; let dry.

3. Punch three snowflake shapes out of metal. Make hole in center of each shape with piercing tool.

4. Pierce three holes in a row along bottom of bag, spacing them evenly. Thread pinwheel charms and snowflakes onto brad prongs; attach brads to bag through punched holes.

5. Glue pompom trim along top edge of bag with hot-glue gun; glue sprig of berries to right side of sheet music.

time-saving tip

Flattening Metal Charms

Punching shapes out of metal is a great way to make your own inexpensive metal charms. The punch usually pinches the edges of the cut design to finish off the edges nicely. To eliminate sharp edges, like the ones the snowflake creates, simply lay the charm flat and pound it with a rubber mallet to flatten it.

Sweetheart Candy

Materials

- ¼" tacky tape
- Candy: sweetheart necklaces (2)
- Eyelet setting tools
- Eyelets: ⅜" aluminum (4)
- Gift bag: 8"x 9½" glossy hot pink
- Ruler

- Scissors
- Sealer: clear protective spray
- Tissue paper: coordinating color (2–3 sheets)
- Wire: 20-gauge nickel or aluminum (48")
- Wire cutters

Instructions

1. Cut off bag handle using scissors. Insert eyelets into handle holes and set with eyelet setting tools.

2. Adhere candy to bag as desired using tacky tape. *Optional:* Seal candy before adhering to the bag by lightly spraying it with clear protective spray and letting it dry.

3. Cut two 24" lengths of wire for handles using wire cutters. On one side of bag, thread 4" of one wire length through one hole of bag from front to back. Bend wire back up and wrap it tightly around itself four times in a close spiral; trim any excess.

4. String candies from one necklace onto wire. Thread opposite end of wire into remaining hole and repeat wire wrapping. Bend handle to desired shape. Repeat on remaining bag handle. Insert gift and add tissue paper to cover.

time-saving tip

To Eat or Not to Eat

It's a good idea to apply a few coats of protective spray to preserve the candy if the gift will be exposed to humidity, heat, or rain. Be sure to warn the recipient that the candy is not to be eaten.

CHAPTER 4

Oddly shaped gifts demand immediate attention because of their unusual form. The ideas in this chapter will help you wrap non-traditional shapes using wallpaper and plastic cylinders, or unusual containers, such as take-out boxes. Many of these vessels also make fabulous wrappings for candies and homemade cookies anytime you want to give someone a little pick-me-up.

Using the wrapping to hint at the contents is not a new idea, but out-of-the-ordinary shapes almost beg to offer the recipient a clue. Present a gift to your new neighbor in a paint can, while a watering can adds just the right touch to a gardening gift for a friend with a green thumb.

Odd Shapes

Take-Out Box

Materials

- Adhesives: glue stick, hot-glue gun
- Beads: green ceramic with large hole, various wood with symbols
- Needle-nose pliers
- Paper: green-and-brown mulberry with writing
- Pencil
- Ribbon: ⅜" brown grosgrain
- Scissors
- Take-out box

Instructions

1. Using pliers, remove wire handles from take-out box and open box completely flat. Lay on wrong side of patterned paper and trace. Cut out and glue to box with glue stick. Fold box back up.

2. Thread wooden beads onto handle, leaving room for them to slide. Reattach handles, using pliers to bend wire back into holes and flattening to secure.

3. Thread ribbon through ceramic bead. Tie around box and secure with hot-glue gun.

time-saving tip

Outside to Backside

Make sure to glue the box template, inside facing up, to the wrong side of the decorative paper. Otherwise, you'll need to fold the box inside out, which can be done but isn't as attractive.

Sweet Treats

Materials

- 1¹⁄₁₆" tacky tape
- Plastic file folder: frosted white
- Ponytail holder with acrylic beads: pink
- Ruler
- Scissors
- Tissue paper: dots, white

Instructions

1. Cut approximately 8" x 11" piece from plastic file folder after cutting off pockets, rings, and finished edges. Place strip of tacky tape on one long edge and wrap into cylinder shape, overlapping opposite edge on top of tacky tape to secure. *Note:* The final cut size will vary, depending on how much of the folder must be cut in order to make a solid piece.

2. Wrap gift in tissue and place inside tube.

3. Wrap white tissue paper around cylinder several times, leaving approximately 3" extending past either end.

4. Cut dot tissue paper to wrap around cylinder once with 3" extending past either end. Wrap and secure with small piece of tacky tape.

5. Secure ends with pink acrylic ponytail holders, forming a wrapped candy shape.

time-saving tip

See-Through Surprise

Office dots, stickers and ribbons also make great decorations for the tubes. Use lengths of decorative ribbons to cover the seam when joining the edges of the tube. After creating your tube, wrap it with clear cellophane instead of tissue to let the contents show through.

Play Clay Box

Materials

- Modeling clay: blue, pink (1 strip each)
- Modeling clay: 5" square (5)
- Plastic box: 5" square
- Ribbon: ¼" blue, pink (5"), 2" green (24")
- Scissors

Instructions

1. Place one square of modeling clay on each side of box, and one square on top. *Note:* Modeling clay is usually purchased in multi-color blocks as shown in this project. If you prefer a different color combination, simply purchase individual colors and form coils to fit your box.

2. Tie green ribbon around box on all four sides; knot ribbon at top. Trim ends at an angle.

3. Tie blue and pink ribbons around knot of green ribbon. Trim ends at an angle.

4. Roll small balls of pink and blue clay. Place along top edge of box on opposite sides; press in place to secure.

5. Roll two long coils of pink and blue clay. Twist two colors together. Place along top edge opposite clay balls.

time-saving tip

A Quick Alternative

If you want to use clay to embellish your box, not cover the entire gift, consider cutting out some shapes with small cookie cutters. Simply press in place to secure.

Patina Purse

Materials

- Acrylic paint: aqua, bronze, teal
- Beads: large (8), small silver (2), spacer (7)
- Needle-nose pliers
- Paintbrushes: artist's detail, foam
- Plastic heart
- Purse handle
- Sea sponges: small pieces (2)
- Wood glue
- Wood purse box

Instructions

1. Unscrew one end of purse handle and string beads on handle, alternating colors. Screw handle back on purse handle.

2. Using foam brush, paint purse box inside and out with teal paint; let dry.

3. Wet one sea sponge; use to apply dabs of bronze paint randomly over teal.

4. Wet second sea sponge; use to apply aqua paint randomly over teal and bronze paint. Touch up randomly with any of the colors until patina effect is achieved.

5. Using detail brush, paint heart embellishment bronze. Adhere embellishment to front center of wood purse box with wood glue.

6. Attach handle to purse by opening wire rings on handle ends, slipping rings over handle brackets on box. Close rings with pliers. Touch up shiny metal on purse handle and brackets with bronze paint.

Home Sweet Home

Materials

- Acrylic paint: blue, red, yellow
- Adhesives: 1$\frac{1}{16}$" tacky tape, hot-glue gun
- Artist's brush
- Cardstock: 12" square golden yellow
- Marker: fine-point black
- Newspaper
- Paint can: gallon size
- Paint stir stick

- Paper plate
- Pencil
- Photos (2)
- Ribbon: $\frac{1}{8}$" blue satin; $\frac{1}{4}$" blue polka dot grosgrain, $\frac{1}{4}$" blue striped, 2" wired fabric
- Ruler
- Scissors
- Tissue paper: blue, off-white

Instructions

1. Cut two 24" lengths of wired fabric ribbon. Set ribbon and paint can on newspaper and squirt out puddles of yellow, blue, and red paint on paper plate. Dip brush in one color and hold over surface; tap brush, causing paint to splatter on entire surface of can. Repeat with remaining colors, one at a time, cleaning brush in between; let dry.

2. Paint first ribbon with various colors and splatter paint on top. Paint second ribbon by dipping end of brush handle in individual paint colors to create random painted dots.

3. Cut two 6" squares of yellow cardstock. Trim corners and adhere one square to each side of paint lid using tacky tape. Adhere before-and-after photos of house, one on each side.

4. Cut two 2$\frac{1}{2}$"x 11" strips of cardstock and join together to make one 21" piece. Adhere around middle of can using tacky tape, overlapping seam in back. Adhere painted ribbon around middle of cardstock with tacky tape. Trim excess where ends meet.

5. Tie shoelace bow with painted polka dot ribbon and adhere to can front with hot-glue gun. Tie various ribbons around left side of handle. Wrap gift in tissue paper and place inside can. Insert stir stick.

Sunflower Watering Can

Materials

- Adhesives: 1¹⁄₁₆" tacky tape, hot-glue gun
- Corrugated cardboard
- Crimper
- Mesh ribbon: 1½" natural
- Metal: 38-gauge aluminum
- Raffia: golden yellow, natural
- Ruler
- Scissors: craft, pinking shears
- Silk sunflower
- String
- Tissue paper
- Wallpaper: yellow gingham
- Watering can

Instructions

1. Measure height and width of each side of watering can from spout to handle. Cut section of wallpaper to fit with pinking shears and adhere to each side.

2. Measure completely around can using string. Cut 4"-wide strip of corrugated cardboard to measured length and adhere using tacky tape around can, through side handle, starting and ending on either side of spout.

3. Cut same length of metal 2½" wide and run through crimper. Center and adhere to corrugated cardboard using tacky tape.

4. Gather several lengths of natural and golden raffia. Tie around can and knot, tying ends in shoelace bow. Secure bow with hot-glue gun.

5. Glue sunflower on top of can. Drape natural mesh ribbon around spout and top of handle; tie off at side of handle.

6. Wrap gift with tissue paper and place inside can.

Foiled Soft Package

Materials

- ¼" tacky tape
- Box
- Craft wire
- Crystal embellishment
- Foil: gold, light metallic blue
- Foiling pen
- Netting: blue/gold metallic
- Scissors
- Tissue paper
- Wallpaper: blue-and-gold flourished pattern

Instructions

1. Measure length of wallpaper to wrap around box. Apply foiling pen to wallpaper pattern, creating accents as desired rather than outlining. Let dry until glue is clear, about 10–20 minutes. Place shiny side of foil on tacky glue; rub and then lift off quickly. *Note:* Foil will stick to glue. Use pieces of both light blue and gold for two-tone effect, applying one right after the other to any missed spots.

2. Wrap wallpaper around empty box using tacky tape, leaving one end of wrapping unsealed.

3. Slide box out and insert tissue-wrapped gift and extra tissue paper as needed to fill in shape; seal end.

4. Wrap netting around package and secure with wire. Add crystal embellishment using wire.

time-saving tip

Large Package Solutions

If your object is too large, or you can't find a box large enough to create a soft package, skip the wallpaper entirely. Use a piece of sturdy cardboard large enough to fit the base of your gift and if desired, embellish it with paint or papers. Use several layers of netting around the cardboard and gather them together at the top. Secure the netting with wire and a decorative tie-on.

Musical Paper Cone

Materials

- Adhesives: ¼" tacky tape, glue stick, hot-glue gun
- Bone folder
- Cardstock: 11½" square
- Garland: berry (24")
- Old sheet music
- Pencil
- Ribbon (16")
- Ruler
- Scissors
- Watercolor paper: 11½" square

Instructions

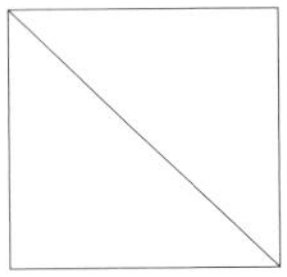

1. Fold cardstock square in half diagonally, forming triangle (Fig. 1). Fold bottom point of triangle up to fold line, making narrower triangle (Fig. 2). Using bone folder, make sharp creases.

Fig. 1

Fig. 2

2. Open the triangle. You will see diagonal lines heading out from lower corner like spokes. Measure 11½" from bottom corner along each spoke line and mark a dot. Connect all dots into an arch from top corner down to bottom right corner (Fig. 3). Cut out and use as pattern.

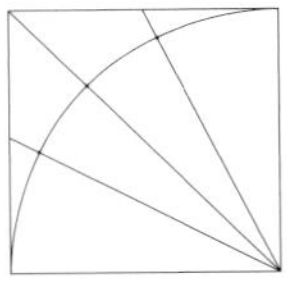

3. Trace pattern onto watercolor paper and cut out. Turn over and glue several sections of old sheet music with glue stick. *Note:* Roll covered paper into cone to see where top will be if you want the sheet music design to face a certain direction.

Fig. 3

4. Roll into cone shape by bringing both edges together, rolling tighter towards tip of cone; adjust and overlap edges as necessary. Once desired cone shape is formed, adhere long edges together using tacky tape.

5. Wrap berry garland in spiral around cone and adhere with hot-glue gun at top and back of cone.

6. Using hot-glue gun, adhere each ribbon end to opposite sides of inside of cone. *Note:* Make sure to center the ribbon handle on each side so that the cone doesn't hang crooked.

CHAPTER 5

No one likes to show up to a party empty-handed. Bottled beverages make the perfect hostess gift, whether to enjoy right away or to save for later. Make your gift extra special—build beaded or wire designs around the bottle itself so the bottle can be used as a vase long after the last drop has been consumed. After seeing how easy it is to cover six-pack carriers, you'll look twice when walking down the grocery aisle. Put a new twist on your gift by using a carrier to present scented spa bottles, mini bottles of wine, or baby bottles for an adorable shower gift. With bottle-wrapping supplies as simple as a plastic file folder and beads and buttons, you'll never show up to an event with a naked bottle again.

Paper Strips

Materials

- Adhesives: craft glue, double-sided tape, quick-dry glue

- Beads: large (2)

- Paper strip: 1"x12", 2"x12" various black designs (12)

- Ribbon: ½" black grosgrain (18")

Instructions

1. Adhere large bead to top of bottle with quick-dry glue.

2. Glue eleven paper strips to each other, allowing a 1" overlap with each new strip, to create 12" square piece of paper using craft glue.

3. Cover bottle on four sides and along bottom edge with double-sided tape.

4. Starting at backside, wrap paper square around bottle. Secure ends of paper with double-sided tape.

5. Tie ribbon into a bow around neck of bottle. Thread each ribbon end through a large bead. Knots ends of ribbon, if necessary.

time-saving tip

Keep Your Scraps

Paper is so fun to work with, and it's often difficult to let go of scraps of your favorite patterns. Keep in mind that leftover strips, squares, and other pieces can be pieced together to make wrapping paper. Papers can also be adhered to a box with decoupage medium to make a permanent wrap.

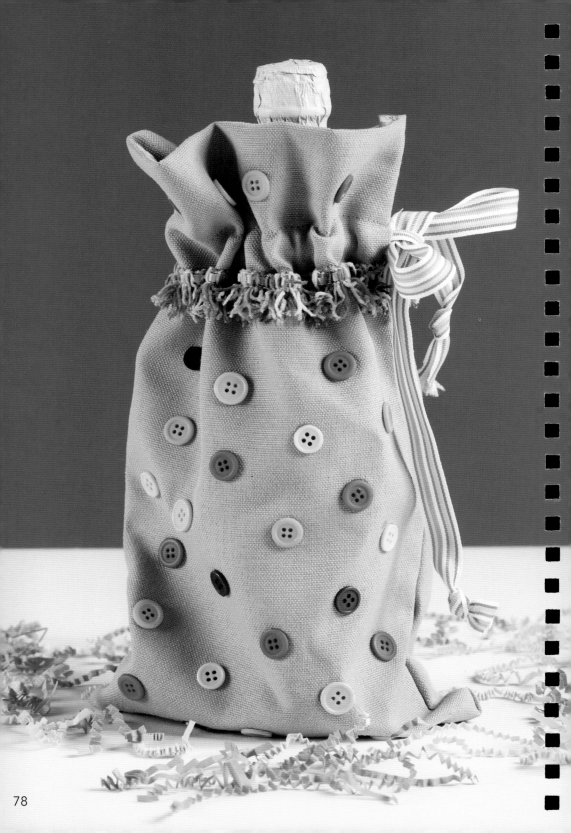

Button Bag

Materials

- Buttons: small assorted colors (60)
- Fabric: 16" square upholstery-weight polyester
- Fabric glue
- Fringe (36")
- Measuring tape
- Ribbon: ½" coordinating striped ribbon (36")
- Ruler
- Safety pin
- Sewing machine and thread
- Straight pins
- Wine or olive oil bottle

Instructions

1. With wrong side of fabric facing up, fold top edge down 3"; pin in place.

2. Measure 1½" from folded top and place straight pins as a guide. Sew line under top row of pins; remove top row of pins.

Fig. 1

Fig. 2

3. Sew along bottom of pinned folded edge, forming casing for ribbon (Fig. 1).

4. Fold in half widthwise. Sew side and bottom using ⅜" seams (Fig. 2). *Note:* Do not sew between the 1" casing.

5. Turn right side out. Glue fringe along outside of bag below casing. Glue buttons on bag in desired pattern; let dry.

6. Attach safety pin to one end of ribbon and thread through casing.

7. Insert bottle in bag and gather ribbon ties around neck, tying to secure.

Ribbon Wrap

Materials

- Adhesives: double-sided tape, glitter adhesive
- Costume jewelry brooch
- Glitter: gold
- Ribbon: ¾" burgundy brocade (18"), 4" burgundy brocade (42")

Instructions

1. Apply glitter adhesive to top of bottle; sprinkle on gold glitter to cover.

2. Cover bottle on four sides and along the bottom with double-sided tape.

3. Place strip of double-sided tape along the selvage edge of 4" ribbon and fold raw edge back over tape to finish edge.

4. Beginning at bottom of bottle with unfinished raw end of ribbon, tightly wrap ribbon around bottle, turning bottle as you work your way up.

5. At top of bottle, gather wide ribbon around neck of bottle. Tie ¾" ribbon around neck. Pin brooch over knot.

time-saving tip

In with the Old

Old costume jewelry makes a lovely adornment on gift wrap, especially for bottles. Brooches, odd earrings, and pendants quickly add glitter and glamour effortlessly.

Baby Boy Six Pack

Materials

- Acrylic paint: sky blue
- Adhesives: ¼" tacky tape, craft glue, fabric glue
- Baby pins: yellow (3)
- Box: 6-pack beverage carton
- Chipboard
- Foam brushes (2)
- Glitter glue: light blue
- Hole punch
- Paper: 12" square various baby patterns (4)
- Ribbon: ½" blue gingham (1 yard), various scraps
- Ruler
- Scissors
- Stamps: baby footprint, baby handprint
- Trim: white pompom (1 yard)
- Wallpaper: paintable embossed

Instructions

1. Measure chipboard to fit box bottom. Cover with tacky tape and adhere to box. Paint entire outside and bottom of carton with blue paint using foam brush.

2. Measure front and back of box. Cut two decorative papers to measured size and adhere with craft glue and clean foam brush. Repeat on side panels. Use different coordinating paper on each side as desired.

3. Measure and cut wallpaper to width of each box end and 3" high. Cut scallops along bottom of each piece's embossed pattern and glue to top of each end of box. Trace around scallops with light blue glitter glue; let dry.

4. Using fabric glue, attach pompom trim to top and blue ribbon to bottom of box around all sides.

5. Using foam brush, apply paint to stamps. Stamp feet and hands randomly on sides of boxes over decorative papers; let dry.

6. Punch holes on one side of handle; thread ribbons through and knot. Attach baby pins as desired. Place baby gifts in each opening.

Bubbly Personality

Materials

- Book board punch and hammer
- Cutting mat
- Eyelet setting tools
- Eyelets: perforated lime green (16)
- File folder: pink plastic
- Glue stick
- Paper punch: 1½" circle
- Photos or magazines
- Piercing tool
- Ribbon: ½" lime sheer organdy (1 yard)
- Ruler
- Scissors
- Wine or olive oil bottle

Instructions

1. Prior to cutting, roll plastic around bottle to check size and adjust as needed. Cut side off pink plastic file folder and trim to 7¼" x 10".

2. Lay plastic flat down on cutting mat and using piercing tool, create eight holes every 1¼" along edge of each side. Insert and set eyelets into holes.

3. Punch circles from photos or magazines, finding fun and interesting colors and images. Adhere randomly to plastic using glue stick.

4. Using book board punch and hammer, punch holes randomly around plastic.

5. Roll plastic into cylinder form. Starting at bottom, insert ribbon into left hole, coming out hole on right side. Center ribbon so equal lengths are hanging out of each hole. Lace ribbon diagonally up cylinder like lacing a shoe, alternating each side across. Slip sleeve over bottle and tighten or loosen laces as needed. Tie ribbon at top in a shoelace bow.

time-saving tip

Holes in the Middle

The arm of a traditional hole punch may not reach the middle of the project's surface. Book board punches can make holes in heavier papers and plastics because of the sharp blade. You can also punch holes anywhere on the project surface by tapping the punch with a hammer.

Wire-Wrapped Design

Materials

- ½" tacky tape
- Needle-nose pliers
- Ruler
- Trim: olivine wired beads (6")
- Wine or olive oil bottle
- Wire: 2mm copper wire (5 yards)
- Wire cutters

Instructions

1. Apply ½" tacky tape around bottom of bottle.

2. Adhere copper wire to tape at back side of bottle bottom. Using hands, wrap wire around bottle in tight coil until tape is completely covered. Continue loosely spiraling wire up around bottle, conforming to shape of bottle. Cut wire and join ends together at top by twisting wire around itself.

3. Grip end of wire with pliers. Using your hand, wrap wire around pliers seven times, stacking it onto itself and forming a flat spiral.

4. Grip wire at end of spiral, and then bend it back in opposite direction, creating a zigzag. Continue bending every 1½" to create five full zigzags, leaving 3" of wire straight.

5. Grip wire with pliers and loop around. Leaving pliers in loop, wrap wire back around itself in tight coil toward zigzags, using other hand. Pull firmly to make tightest coil possible. Cut off wire at end with wire cutters. Repeat two more times to create three large charms.

6. Attach charms randomly on spiral-wrapped bottle by tucking zigzags and coils under or over spiraled wire to secure. Mold charms around bottle. Cut sections from olivine-beaded trim and dangle from wire-wrapped charms.

time-saving tip

Dress It Up

Instead of creating your own wire-wrapped charms, use old jewelry or interesting metal charms. Secure with wire or jump rings in various spots on the spiral-wrapped bottle.

Star Catcher

Materials

- Charms: gold stars (21)
- Glittered netting: 8"
- Jump rings (21)
- Needle-nose pliers (2)
- Ribbon: ¼" sheer antique brown (8")
- Scissors
- Wine or olive oil bottle
- Wire: 26-gauge aluminum (4")
- Wire cutters

Instructions

1. Cut length of netting long enough to wrap approximately 3" over bottle top. Secure netting around neck of bottle with wire, tucking edges to back side of bottle.

2. Pull each corner of ragged edges of top of netting up and over top of bottle, pulling neck of bottle through netting grid. Repeat with remaining corners that are sticking up, creating a fancy poof.

3. Holding needle-nose pliers in each hand, open jump ring and insert into star charm loop. Attach jump ring to netting and close, securing charm. Repeat with remaining charms, placing randomly around netting. Tie ribbon into bow around center of bottle.

time-saving tip

Opening Jump Rings

Always open a jump ring by twisting the circle open, rather than by straightening it. Using two pairs of pliers, hold each side of the ring with the opening on top. Twist the right side of the circle backward, while twisting the left side of the circle forward. This will maintain the circular shape of the jump ring and allow you to twist it back together so that it is joined as tightly as possible.

Beaded Beauty

Materials

- Adhesives: ⅛" tacky tape, ½" tacky tape, craft glue
- Beads: black seed, gold micro
- Inkpad: gold pigment
- Plastic containers (2)
- Rhinestones: 4mm assorted red, black flat-back
- Ribbon: ⅝" red satin, 1½" red mesh
- Sealing wax and seal
- Wine bottle

Instructions

1. Outline bottle label with ½" tacky tape. Peel off tape liner to reveal sticky part of tape and place rhinestones randomly on tape as desired.

2. Holding bottle over plastic container, sprinkle black seed beads over tape. Repeat with gold micro beads and remaining container until all exposed tape is covered.

3. Using craft glue, adhere red mesh ribbon around top of bottle's neck. Wrap ⅛" tacky tape around top and bottom of mesh ribbon. Cover tape as in Step 2, using gold micro beads.

4. Wrap 12" length of red satin ribbon around shoulders of bottle. Press brass seal onto gold pigment ink pad to coat. Drip circle of wax where ribbon intersects, wait about three seconds, and then press brass seal into wax. Hold until wax hardens and then remove.

time-saving tip

Wax Seals Made Easy

Traditional sealing wax comes in blocks with wicks and usually dries brittle, causing it to crack over time. Sealing wax sticks can be used with a low-temp glue gun to create seals quickly. This method means a more controllable flow of wax and the elimination of the need to light a wick. As a bonus, the polymer added to these wax sticks also makes the wax suppler so it doesn't crack.

CHAPTER 6

Gift cards will be a whole lot more fun to give using the projects in this chapter. Imagine granting a birthday girl's wish with a magical wand or handing a work colleague a caffeinated thank you. A mom-to-be would appreciate a gift card to a baby boutique, and an embellished box is an adorable holder for suggestions of the things to be purchased for the little one.

Make your own personalized coupons for your special sweetheart and present them in an accordion-style book for a birthday or anniversary gift. Any gift card needs a touch of personality and a fancy, easy-to-make sleeve fits the bill. Once you learn how to add a few simple touches to a gift card, you'll always be able to show the extra consideration that you put into the gift.

Holiday Surprise

Materials

- Adhesives: ¼" tacky tape, glue stick
- Chipboard pieces: 1¾" square (2), 1¾" x 2¾" (1)
- Cord: gold (24")
- Embossing powder: gold
- Heat gun
- Inkpad: gold pigment
- Leafing pen: gold

- Marker: fine-point black
- Note card with envelope: 6½" x 4½"
- Paper: 4" square burgundy-and-gold marbled (2), 3¾" x 5" gold vellum
- Ribbon: ⅝" gold-edged sheer burgundy (8")
- Rubber stamp: snowflakes
- Scissors

Instructions

1. Create gift card sleeve using Sleeve Diagram and gold vellum (Fig. 1).

2. Apply glue stick to side flap. Fold opposite side over and attach to flap. Apply glue stick to bottom flap and fold up to close bottom of sleeve.

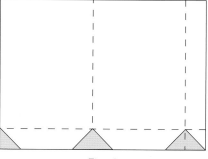

Fig. 1

3. Wrap marbled paper around chipboard squares and adhere. Wrap gold cord around a wrapped square and tie in a shoelace bow. Repeat with remaining wrapped square.

4. Adhere vellum gift card sleeve to large chipboard piece. Tie shoelace bow using ribbon and adhere to card sleeve. Adhere sleeve and wrapped squares to card front using tacky tape.

5. Stamp snowflakes on note card using gold inkpad. Sprinkle with gold embossing powder and melt with heat gun. Color edges using gold leafing pen. Insert gift card into sleeve on card front and write message inside card.

Valentine CD Holder

Materials

- Bone folder
- Cardstock: 12" square red kraft
- CD
- CD holder: cardboard
- Embossed foil borders: gold
- Foil: gold, red
- Foiling pen

- Glue stick
- Inkpad: black waterproof
- Paper: 12" square patterned
- Rubber stamp: 3½" heart
- Ruler
- Scissors

Instructions

1. Stamp heart on red cardstock with black inkpad; cut out. Apply foiling pen in swirled design on heart; let dry to become tacky and clear, about 15–20 minutes. Once dry, apply red foil shiny side up; press down and then peel off quickly, leaving foil accents on glued areas.

2. Carefully open CD holder where it is glued together on flaps and flatten. Adhere front of holder to back side of patterned paper with glue stick and trim excess paper. Adhere kraft cardstock to inside of holder and trim excess.

3. Re-trace scored lines of holder with ruler and bone folder. Re-fold holder and glue flaps back together with glue stick.

4. Randomly swipe holder cover with glue stick. Immediately press gold foil on glue and lift off, leaving random foil designs; repeat as desired on front and back.

5. Using glue stick, apply gold-embossed foil borders to front cover, wrapping around to the inside. Adhere foiled heart to center of cover.

6. Rub black inkpad along top of inside edge.

7. Create card to match using remaining paper and cardstock; insert gift card into right side of holder. Insert personalized CD into sleeve on left side.

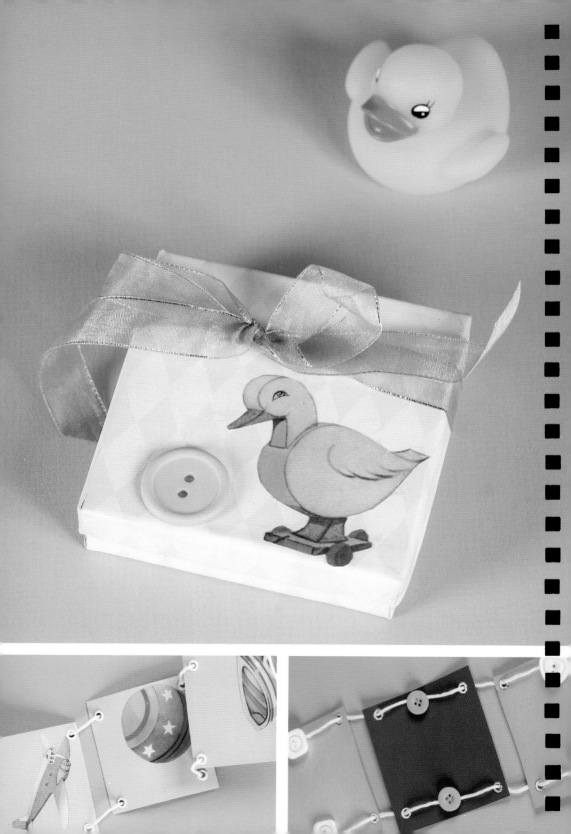

Toy Box

Materials

- Adhesives: $\frac{1}{4}$" tacky tape, glue stick, hot-glue gun
- Box: $3\frac{1}{2}$" square
- Button: 1" yellow, $\frac{5}{8}$" white (8)
- Cardstock: $3\frac{1}{4}$"x $6\frac{1}{2}$" light blue, yellow (1 each)
- Eyelet setting tools
- Eyelets: $\frac{3}{8}$" white (16)
- Paper: 12" square harlequin patterned, decorative wrapping paper with vintage toys (1 each)
- Pencil
- Ribbon: $\frac{5}{8}$" gold-edged sheer turquoise
- Ruler
- Scissors
- String (50")

Instructions

1. Cut $5\frac{1}{2}$" square harlequin paper. Cover box lid with glue stick and place in center of back side of paper. With ruler and pencil, draw line from bottom right corner down to edge of paper. Repeat with following corners: top corner of right edge, left corner of top edge, and bottom corner of left edge. Trim paper with scissors on pencil lines. Apply glue stick to flaps and fold up edge of box and around corners, each side overlapping the next.

2. Cut two $3\frac{1}{4}$" squares each of yellow and light blue cardstock. Insert white eyelets in each corner of each square. Cut toy images out of wrapping paper and glue to bottom right of each square.

3. Cut two 25" lengths of string. Thread cards together and tie in shoelace bow at top and bottom. Adhere two buttons on back of each card to secure string.

4. Adhere top card to inside lid of box with two strips of tacky tape.

5. Glue image to top of box using glue stick. Glue button to top of box using hot-glue gun; insert gift card. Wrap sheer ribbon around box and tie in a shoelace bow.

Fun Frame

Materials

- Acrylic paint: cobalt teal, medium violet
- Adhesives: clear glitter glue, dimensional glossy glue, glue stick
- Foam brushes (2)
- Paper: floral print (1), coordinating patterned papers (2)
- Paper punch: 1" daisy
- Photo corners: coordinating color (4)
- Rhinestones: 4mm assorted colors (8)
- Ruler
- Scissors
- Wood frame: 5" x 7"

Instructions

1. Remove glass from frame and paint frame cobalt teal. Brush medium violet paint along inside and outside edges. Cut out six flower shapes from floral print paper. Punch four different flowers from same paper.

2. Glue flowers along bottom left corner and upper right corner of frame with glue stick in desired pattern.

3. Squeeze glitter glue onto scrap paper. Using clean foam brush, paint glitter glue onto frame; let dry.

4. Adhere rhinestones inside several flowers with dimensional glue. Dot glitter glue in center of other flowers; let dry.

5. Cut coordinating paper to fit frame opening. Cut 3½" x 2¼" piece of second coordinating paper to fit gift card. Attach photo corners and adhere to center of larger paper; insert gift card. Replace glass and insert paper into frame. Replace frame back.

time-saving tip

Two Gifts in One

This project is a perfect example of two gifts in one. Coordinate the colors of the frame with the recipient's home décor. Once the gift card has been removed, the frame can hold a treasured photo. If you don't have a gift card, simply mat and frame cold, hard cash. Any teenager will appreciate your generosity.

Coffee Bean Cup

Materials

- Adhesives: ¼" tacky tape, glue stick
- Coffee beans (1 cup)
- Corrugated sleeve
- Foam cup with lid: 5¼"
- Inkpad: brown
- Marker: fine-point black
- Paper: coordinating colors and patterns (2)
- Ribbon: ⅝" black grosgrain (32")
- Rubber stamp: coffee bean
- Ruler
- Scissors
- Shipping tag: 1⅜" x 1¾" kraft
- Tissue paper: 2½" x 9½" kraft circle

Instructions

1. Cut eight 1¼" x 5¼" strips of patterned papers. Glue strips vertically side by side at top of cup, overlapping strips to make it seem as if paper is tapered.

2. Adhere corrugated sleeve around middle of cup with tacky tape. Fold tissue paper in half lengthwise, wrap around center of sleeve and secure with glue.

3. Fill cup with coffee beans, insert gift card, and place lid on top. Wrap ribbon around cup and knot on top of lid.

4. Stamp shipping tag with coffee bean stamp and write message. Tie onto ribbon tail.

time-saving tip

Coffee Bean Surprise

Many coffee houses will give you a cup full of beans at no charge when you purchase their gift cards. In addition, the cup sleeve can be turned inside out for an instant corrugated trim.

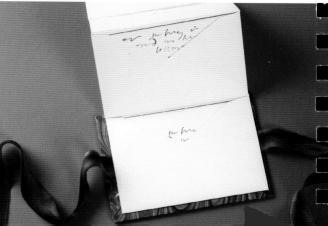

Accordion Envelope Book

Materials

- Bone folder
- Chipboard: 4"x 5½" (2)
- Envelopes: 3⅝"x 5⅛" white (5)
- Glue stick
- Paper: 12" square patterned
- Ribbon: ½" hand-dyed silk coordinating color (18")
- Ruler
- Scissors

Instructions

1. Apply glue stick to inside of one envelope flap and attach it to back of a second envelope. Make sure not to cover crease line. Repeat with remaining envelopes. Fold envelopes like an accordion, so that bottom of stack is smooth and stack ends with flap on top.

2. Cut two 4"x 5½" pieces of chipboard and two 5"x 6½" pieces of paper. Apply glue stick thoroughly to one chipboard piece and place in center back side of one piece of paper. Smooth paper onto board with bone folder, eliminating all wrinkles. Repeat with remaining chipboard and paper pieces.

3. Crease paper at corners by folding up to edge of chipboard. Trim to ⅛" before crease line on all four corners to get rid of excess paper when wrapping. Apply glue to long sides of paper and board. Wrap paper tightly around chipboard. Taper corners of side flaps and apply glue completely to each side edge. Wrap around chipboard tightly.

4. Choose board for bottom of book and lay it wrong side up. Fold ribbon in half to determine center. Unfold and adhere center of ribbon horizontally across center of chipboard. Glue stack of envelopes on top of ribbon. Fold flap of top envelope forward and apply glue to it. Note: To make sure you don't get glue on the rest of the envelope, insert a paper scrap under flap.

5. Adhere remaining piece of chipboard on top of stack, right side facing up. Cut 5¼" x 3¾" piece of paper. Glue to inside cover, covering flap. Insert gift cards, handmade coupons, or photos in pockets. Tie ribbon in shoelace bow to close.

Marbled Gift Tin

Materials

- Alcohol inks: gold metallic, lettuce, plum
- Bookplate: 2⅝" x 1¼" antique brass
- Felt applicator
- Glossy paper: 2" x 3" white
- Leafing pen: gold
- Marker: fine-point black
- Mini brads: antique brass (2)
- Mint tin: 2¼" x 3¾"
- Piercing tool
- Ribbon: 1" lime sheer (18")
- Ruler
- Scissors

Instructions

1. Add five drops of plum and metallic gold alcohol ink to felt applicator. Sponge onto lid and bottom of tin, alternating direction each time until desired color and pattern is achieved.

2. Center bookplate on lid and pierce holes with piercing tool. Insert mini brads to secure bookplate to lid.

3. Using gold leafing pen, color hinges and lip of lid.

4. With new piece of felt, add five drops of lettuce and metallic gold ink to applicator. Apply to small piece of glossy paper; let dry. Cut paper to approximately 1" x 2". Write recipient's name or sentiment on center of paper and insert into bookplate.

5. Place gift card inside tin and tie ribbon horizontally to close. Trim tails as desired.

time-saving tip

Tantalizing Tins

A variety of tin containers can be found in all sorts of unexpected places, such as garage sales, antique stores, candy aisles, and even the favor aisle of party stores. Small tins that aren't large enough for a card can hold a picture of something special to purchase with the card.

Fairy Wand

Materials

- Acrylic paint: silver
- Adhesives: dimensional glossy glue, hot-glue gun
- Bone folder
- Brads: silver (2)
- Craft knife
- Dowel: ⅜" (22")
- Florist wire: 26-gauge aluminum (1 yard)
- Foam brush
- Mica flakes

- Papier-mâché star with eyelet holes: 7" white
- Pencil
- Piercing tool
- Ribbons: 1" bias-cut hand-dyed peach silk (1 yard), 2" sheer ivory (24"), ½" blue vintage fabric (28")
- Ruler
- Scissors
- Trims: silver cord (24"), ivory fiber (24")
- Vintage image: 2" x 3"

Instructions

1. Paint dowel rod with several coats of silver paint using foam brush; let dry between applications.

2. Using craft knife, cut around top arm of star and down 3½" on each side forming door. Use ruler and bone folder to score door bottom.

3. Brush dimensional glossy glue over star front. Lay image on star center. Sprinkle mica flakes around image, covering star completely. Let dry 10–15 minutes and then brush off excess flakes. Repeat on back side.

time-saving tip

Seeing Stars

Fairy stars also look great as hanging plaques. Simply loop a ribbon through the existing eyelet holes and tie with a shoelace bow. Your recipient can hang the star on the wall or a doorknob. The plaque can also be set on top of other gifts as a wrapping decoration and hold an extra surprise.

Above: Insert gift card inside the door on the back of the Fairy Wand.

4. Pierce holes in each side of door, ½" inside edges; be sure to line up with pre-made holes. Insert large brad in each pierced hole and bend prongs to inside of door.

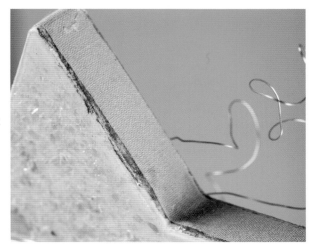

Above: Vintage ribbon on the star's edge.

5. Cut hole in bottom center of star with craft knife. Insert dowel and secure with hot glue. Wrap 36" length of silk ribbon around wand, securing with dimensional glue at wand top and bottom. Glue vintage ribbon around star edge, beginning at star bottom. Wrap lengths of remaining ribbons and trims around wand.

6. Fold 36" wire length in half. From front of star, insert folded wire edge through left hole and out back hole. Insert other half of wire through right hole and out back. Insert gift card. Twist wire ends around brads to secure door.

7. Cut folded edge of wire and separate into two different ends. Curl all wire ends around pencil forming spirals.

time-saving tip
Dimensional Glue Uses

Usually glossy dimensional glue is used to create raised, glass-like domes over images and words. Because it dries quickly, brush it on your project to hold mica flakes. Its glossy finish won't detract from the sparkling flakes like most clear glues would.

CHAPTER 7

When all is bought and wrapped, you're almost ready to give the gift away. But before you do, take a moment to create a unique finishing touch with a gift tag. It's important to match the style of the tag to the occasion. There are floral tags for springtime gifts that look great on rustic kraft paper or beautiful, hand-painted papers; others use crystals for an elegant look on wedding and special occasion gifts. Tags also make great gifts. Craft a charming tag that can be worn later as a pendant or saved as a nostalgic keepsake ornament. For an earthy touch, use distressed materials to complement a masculine or nautical theme. No matter which idea you choose, these gift tags are sure to become mementos treasured long after the wrapping has been discarded.

113

Distressed Pocket

Materials

- Adhesives: ¼" tacky tape, hot-glue gun
- Buttons: assorted coordinating colors and patterns (3)
- Inkpads: distressed green, distressed brown
- Iron
- Ribbon: ½" green stripe twill (6½"), ½" orange-and-green stripe twill (6½")
- Ruler
- Scissors: fabric, pinking shears
- Shipping tags: 3⅛" x 6¼" kraft, 1⅜" x 2¾" manila
- Spray bottle with water
- String (6")

Instructions

1. Crumple kraft tag. Open and rub distressed green inkpad over tag, coloring all wrinkles. Mist inked tag lightly with water to spread color. Press flat with iron.

2. Trim bottom edge of tag using pinking shears and fold up toward top of tag, ending approximately ½" below hole. Rub around outside edges using brown inkpad.

3. Wrap two lines of tacky tape, 1" apart, around tag to secure pocket closed on sides. Remove tape liner and cover with ribbon, joining ends on the back side; trim excess ribbon.

4. Glue buttons to front using hot glue. Add ribbon to top hole and tie onto gift.

5. Write message or name on manila tag using black marker. Add string and slide into pocket.

time-saving tip

Plain or Patterned Pockets

To make a fast pocket, simply fold the shipping tag without distressing it and then use any trim or ribbon you have handy. Adhere the pocket directly onto your gift using double-sided tape. Pockets can also hold gift cards. Simply attach the card using a dimensional glue dot so it doesn't fall out.

Flower Pebble

Materials

- Adhesives: foam dots, hot-glue gun, tacky tape sheet
- Flower: 4½" silk coordinating color
- Glass pebble: ½" clear
- Marker: fine-point black
- Paper: coordinating color
- Pencil
- Scissors

Instructions

1. Write initials or recipient's name on paper.

2. Trace glass pebble on paper and tacky tape; cut out. Adhere paper cutout to back of pebble using tacky tape cutout.

3. Remove center of silk flower. Glue center of flower layers together using small amount of hot glue.

4. Adhere pebble to flower center using tacky tape. Attach to gift using several foam dots.

time-saving tip

Wearable Wishes

If you are looking for a way to focus the spotlight on the birthday girl and let everyone know it's her special day, look no further. Insert a birthday message under the pebble and adhere a pin clasp to the back. Pin it on the gift and invite her to wear it all day long.

Rhinestone Dog Tag

Materials

- Alcohol ink: plum
- Ball chain (24")
- Brad: square fuchsia
- Charms: aluminum monogram, pinwheel
- Dog tag: 2½" x 1⅝" aluminum
- Felt applicator
- Rhinestones: olivine (6), pink (2)
- Strong-hold glue
- Trim: scrap denim with steel rings
- Tweezers
- Wire cutters

Instructions

1. Adhere piece of denim trim diagonally across dog tag using glue.

2. Paint monogram plum using alcohol ink and felt applicator; let dry.

3. Grip pinwheel with tweezers, dip charm back in glue, and place on tag as desired. Repeat with rhinestones, placing pink rhinestone in pinwheel center and olivine rhinestones randomly around pinwheel.

4. Trim brad prongs using wire cutters. Adhere brad to dog tag.

5. Adhere pink monogram and pink rhinestone at top corner. Let dry at least 30 minutes or overnight, if possible. Thread chain through tag before attaching to gift.

time-saving tip

Choosing Metal Glue

Non-toxic metal glue works like super glue but without the fumes. Don't worry if the adhesive shows around the charms or rhinestones. Apply it as carefully as you can and after it dries, gently rub off any excess spots with a cotton swab soaked in rubbing alcohol.

Glass Charm

Materials

- Cosmetic sponge
- Fern: natural or silk
- Glass squares: 1½" square (2)
- Inkpad: brown
- Marker: fine-point black
- Memory frame: 1½" square
- Ribbon: ⅛" green variegated (24")
- Vellum paper scrap

Instructions

1. Tear strip of vellum paper smaller than glass size; write name or message on paper. Sponge outside edges using brown ink.

2. Sandwich fern and message between glass squares. Wrap memory frame around glass, securing according to manufacturer's instructions.

3. Thread ribbon through top of frame and tie to gift.

time-saving tip

Giving Tags as Gifts

Create a photo collage pendant that is a means of identifying the recipient and also serves as a gift itself. Simply cut paper the same size as the glass charm for a background. Add miniature photos, stamped images, words, flat charms, and glitter glue. If you don't have a memory frame on hand, wrap metal tape around the outside and glue on a jewelry bail with a loop at the top; add a jump ring and string onto a pretty chain.

Metal-Rimmed Tag

Materials

- Glue stick
- Metal-rimmed tag: 2¼"
- Mini brad: yellow
- Paper flowers: large yellow, small white
- Pencil
- Pinking shears
- Ribbon: ¼" black-and-white gingham (6")
- Studs: initials
- Wallpaper scrap

Instructions

1. Trace metal-rimmed tag twice onto wallpaper scrap. Cut inside traced lines using pinking shears.

2. Layer flowers and attach to one circle using mini brad.

3. Attach initial studs to remaining circle. Flatten prongs to back side.

4. Adhere circle to each side of tag using glue stick.

5. Add ribbon and tie onto gift.

Metal-Embossed Monogram

Materials

- Adhesives: ¼" tacky tape, glue stick
- Alphabet stencil: (2")
- Charm: glittered flower
- Chipboard: 8½" x 11"
- Crystal spear with gold finding
- Crystal strand (2")
- Foam mat
- Glitter glue: silver
- Metal sheet: 38-gauge aluminum (3¾")
- Mirror: ½" round
- Paper: antique sheet music
- Piercing tool
- Ribbon: ¼" sheer ivory (6")
- Ruler
- Scissors
- Stylus tool

Instructions

1. Cut 3¼" chipboard square and 3¾" square of sheet music using scissors. Center and adhere paper on chipboard using glue stick, wrapping edges onto back. Cut 3" square of sheet music and adhere to back, covering raw edges.

2. Cut 3¾" square of aluminum metal and lay on foam mat. Reverse alphabet stencil and center letter on metal square. Trace inside stencil using stylus, pushing metal into foam to emboss. Turn metal over and place on hard, smooth surface. Trace with stylus on either side of embossed line to create a crisp, defined line.

3. Cut 2¾" chipboard square. Center and adhere to back of embossed metal using tacky tape. Wrap metal around chipboard.

4. Wrap sheer ribbon around top of metal charm and adhere on back side. Adhere glittered flower charm to top left corner. Adhere mirror to center of flower.

5. Attach metal square to sheet music square using tacky tape.

6. Make hole ½" below top corner and ½" above bottom corner using piercing tool. Attach strand of crystals to top hole and dangle crystal spear from bottom hole. Brush inside of monogram with glitter glue; let dry. Tie to gift using ribbon.

Chandelier Crystal

Materials

- Adhesives: dimensional glossy glue, glue stick
- Chandelier crystal with gold finding
- Foil: gold
- Leafing pen: gold
- Marker: fine-point black
- Paper scrap
- Pencil
- Ribbon: narrow
- Scissors

Instructions

1. Trace crystal onto paper using pencil. Write name inside shape using black marker. Cut out with pinking shears and adhere to back of crystal using dimensional glossy glue.

2. Apply glue stick to back of crystal randomly. Press foil down on glue and lift up.

3. Color edges of crystal with gold leafing pen; let dry.

4. Tie crystal to gift using ribbon.

time-saving tip

Photo Pendants

A velvet ribbon can turn a clever tag into a fancy choker. Instead of adhering names to the back, use pictures or create a collage. These embellished crystals also make beautiful ornaments during the holidays. Make sure to test your inks before gluing as some may smear.

Antique Optical Lens

Materials

- Adhesives: dimensional glossy glue, glue stick
- Foil: gold
- Jump ring
- Marker: fine-point black
- Needle-nose pliers
- Optical lens with open hole
- Paper scrap
- Pencil
- Ribbon: narrow
- Scissors

Instructions

1. Trace circle of optical lens onto paper twice and cut out.

2. Write message or name on paper scrap and cut out. Adhere to paper circle using glue stick.

3. Apply glue stick around lens edges; press foil shiny side up on glue and then lift up.

4. Apply glossy glue to printed circle and press onto back of optical lens so that design shows through the front.

5. Adhere remaining paper circle to back of previous circle using glue stick. Antique with foil as in Step 3.

6. Attach jump ring to hole at top of lens using needle-nose pliers. Tie to gift using ribbon.

time-saving tip

Looking for Lenses

Optical lenses have become a treasured item for mixed media and altered art artists. If the local art store doesn't have them, you can easily find lenses online and you can choose the design and metal color. Inexpensive replicas work well for tags, although fancier ones make great keepsake pendants.

About the Author

Based in the Santa Ana Artists Village in Southern California, Nicole Ann Steiman has been facilitating creativity seminars for more than twelve years in both corporate and retail environments. Her passionate love for paper is what drove her to create The ARTbar Studio, with the mission to provide a place for everyone to experience art. Her background as a trainer, along with her current mixed media art career, has helped her take even complicated art techniques and break them down into easy-to-learn projects. Nicole firmly believes that everyone can be an artist, and that it starts with adding creativity to the everyday things we do. www.theartbar.net

Acknowledgments

I am grateful for my large, loving, and very creative family, who provides countless opportunities for outdoing each other with cleverly wrapped gifts.

I dedicate this book to the following special people in my life:

To Rachel Williams, ARTbar manager, for her endless energy and all-knowing sense of style. You are a designer extraordinaire!

To all The ARTbar customers who excused the blown-up look of the studio and happily created in the chaos anyway.

To my fabulous consultant team and artist contributors:

Kathleen Ames, painter of the most beautiful wrapping papers. Who ever thought kraft paper could get any better?

Marian Ballog, an artist with an endless river of clever ideas.

Erica Batchelder, creator of the most beautiful hand-dyed silk ribbons.

Cindy at Wallpapers To Go in Mission Viejo, for fabulous "waterproof wrapping papers."

Joyce Carlson, who can brainstorm the heck out of any topic, especially "Button Bottle Bags."

Sherry Goodloe, who has an eye for turning all things into art, especially "Baby Six Pack" carriers.

Eileen Paulin for believing in me at first sight.

Jenna Ryan, the Cupcake Queen of Inspiration and Kraft Paper Goddess.

My daughter, Josie Steiman, who makes me look at everything a little bit differently. At age 3 you are already an artist. Don't ever forget it.

And most of all, I dedicate this book to my husband and soul-twin, Mark Steiman, who believes I can do anything. And with a love like his, who couldn't?

METRIC EQUIVALENCY CHARTS

inches to millimeters and centimeters
(mm-millimeters, cm-centimeters)

inches	mm	cm	inches	cm	inches	cm
1/8	3	0.3	9	22.9	30	76.2
1/4	6	0.6	10	25.4	31	78.7
1/2	13	1.3	12	30.5	33	83.8
5/8	16	1.6	13	33.0	34	86.4
3/4	19	1.9	14	35.6	35	88.9
7/8	22	2.2	15	38.1	36	91.4
1	25	2.5	16	40.6	37	94.0
1 1/4	32	3.2	17	43.2	38	96.5
1 1/2	38	3.8	18	45.7	39	99.1
1 3/4	44	4.4	19	48.3	40	101.6
2	51	5.1	20	50.8	41	104.1
2 1/2	64	6.4	21	53.3	42	106.7
3	76	7.6	22	55.9	43	109.2
3 1/2	89	8.9	23	58.4	44	111.8
4	102	10.2	24	61.0	45	114.3
4 1/2	114	11.4	25	63.5	46	116.8
5	127	12.7	26	66.0	47	119.4
6	152	15.2	27	68.6	48	121.9
7	178	17.8	28	71.1	49	124.5
8	203	20.3	29	73.7	50	127.0

yards to meters

yards	meters	yards	meters	yards	meters	yards	meters	yards	meters
1/8	0.11	2 1/8	1.94	4 1/8	3.77	6 1/8	5.60	8 1/8	7.43
1/4	0.23	2 1/4	2.06	4 1/4	3.89	6 1/4	5.72	8 1/4	7.54
3/8	0.34	2 3/8	2.17	4 3/8	4.00	6 3/8	5.83	8 3/8	7.66
1/2	0.46	2 1/2	2.29	4 1/2	4.11	6 1/2	5.94	8 1/2	7.77
5/8	0.57	2 5/8	2.40	4 5/8	4.23	6 5/8	6.06	8 5/8	7.89
3/4	0.69	2 3/4	2.51	4 3/4	4.34	6 3/4	6.17	8 3/4	8.00
7/8	0.80	2 7/8	2.63	4 7/8	4.46	6 7/8	6.29	8 7/8	8.12
1	0.91	3	2.74	5	4.57	7	6.40	9	8.23
1 1/8	1.03	3 1/8	2.86	5 1/8	4.69	7 1/8	6.52	9 1/8	8.34
1 1/4	1.14	3 1/4	2.97	5 1/4	4.80	7 1/4	6.63	9 1/4	8.46
1 3/8	1.26	3 3/8	3.09	5 3/8	4.91	7 3/8	6.74	9 3/8	8.57
1 1/2	1.37	3 1/2	3.20	5 1/2	5.03	7 1/2	6.86	9 1/2	8.69
1 5/8	1.49	3 5/8	3.31	5 5/8	5.14	7 5/8	6.97	9 5/8	8.80
1 3/4	1.60	3 3/4	3.43	5 3/4	5.26	7 3/4	7.09	9 3/4	8.92
1 7/8	1.71	3 7/8	3.54	5 7/8	5.37	7 7/8	7.20	9 7/8	9.03
2	1.83	4	3.66	6	5.49	8	7.32	10	9.14

INDEX